G000075544

Reading as a Social Action:
Women Aspiring for More

Volume I

Tammy C. Francis, Ph.D., Editor

Paperback ISBN: 978-1-7355609-2-2
eBook ISBN: 978-1-7355609-3-9

T. F. Donaldson Global Enterprise, LLC
Catalyst 4 Change Global, LLC
www.catalyst4changeglobal.net
DrTammy@catalyst4changeglobal.net

Dedication

To Elizabeth, Brianna and Sanaa.

To all the women who have found themselves in a situation or transition that interrupted their flow toward more.

To all the women who despite what life handed them made lemonade…and kept going.

To my co-authors and friends, Jeanine Bunzigiye, Chipo Chitewe, Ruth-Ellen Danquah, LaShun Gaines, Lynn Kanyowa-Ndhlovu, Shawntai Lister-Mitchell, and D. Trifanya Osei, who have supported my platform, brand, and vision from the beginning, thank you! You ladies make being a woman aspiring for more easier to move in the direction of more and prepare for what's next. The grace you have given me over the years is amazing. Thank you for believing in me and never giving up on my mission and vision.

To all the women aspiring for more!

Also by Dr. Tammy

Manifesting More: A Playbook for Planning and Living on Purpose

R.E.A.P. More: 76 Seeds for This Season

Chapters and Collaborations

Social Media as a 21st Century Playground
(in "Play in American Life" by Mary Ruth Moore and Constance Sabo-Risley, editors)

Remove the Limits
(in "Stronger: A Guide for Women Entrepreneurs on Finding Hope and Motivation for Business During Times of Crisis")

Flow
(in "You Can: 33 Stories to Uplift & Inspire Everyday People" compiled by Nina Motivates)

Table of Contents

Reading as a Social Action

Preface

These are stories from the women actively engaged in a global, online reading community called *Women Aspiring for More (WAM)*. I launched the reading community in May 2017. It was set up as an engaging space to build relationships, educate each other, and serve others. WAM was established to encourage reading, promote self-awareness, and invest in self-development through literature and literacy.

WAM pushes women toward knowledge, light, and self-awareness and serves as a catalyst for personal change. WAM actively supports and celebrates women to walk in their passion, step into their purpose, and live in both spaces comfortably and intentionally. This self-work is grounded in literary catalysis, the interaction within the reading community for personal and professional development.

There are women from all around the world in this community. These stories are just a sampling of the women from different parts of the world—Congo, London, and United States. In their chapters, you will also see them written in the English dialect of their geographical region, whether it is vocabulary, pronunciation, spelling, or grammar. It was my attempt to not change their words to fit standard American English, but to let their authentic voices share their reading experiences. So, you will note the nuances and authenticity in each author's chapter.

In this anthology, the women share their experiences and stories about using reading as a vehicle to grow personally and professionally while in a community reading with like-minded women and engaging in conversations from different perspectives. Each contributor shares how reading with others in WAM has changed their reading habits, reading experience(s), reading enjoyment, and/or attitude toward reading.

The contributors are Jeanine Bunzigiye, Chipo Chitewe, Ruth-Ellen Danquah, LaShun Gaines, Lynn Kanyowa-Ndhlovu, Shawntai Lister-Mitchell, and Trifanya Osei.

There is also an art piece included. Initially, I had a different idea for how I would use an original art piece by my nephew, artist, actor, and creator, Marcus Humose. Now years later, I have decided not to use it for the cover; but I have found a better and more perfect place for it in the *Afterword.*

Years? Yes. This book has taken me years to complete, publish. Initially, when I sent out the call for this book, it was time, and I was excited about doing it and getting it done. Then life happened. I was going through a real challenging time personally, and it shook up my life. Then when I thought, "I need to finish it!" I no longer had that feeling, "it was time" to complete. It never felt like the time to do it. I went back and forth about whether or not to refund the ladies their money and scrap the project all together or go forward. Never was that the answer—to cancel the project. The answer was not yet, but something I needed to do and complete.

The contributors, my co-author, were patient with me and this transition process. Some of them would check on me and the progress. It was difficult to explain to them that "it wasn't" time to release—no matter how much I needed to fulfill my promise to them and how I desired so to share our stories with the world. However, they did not push or give me a difficult time about it. They were the most patient co-authors and friends. Thank you! It means the world to me that you trusted me with your stories, your money, and your goals. This has definitely been a labor of love, but not in the traditional sense, like the time it took to complete, but in the faith, hope, and love shown toward me by my co-authors and friends as I navigated through my growing pains, my journey toward more.

Now, I share them with you. Look to be inspired, encouraged, empowered, and equipped to move in the direction of more and prepare for what's next.

Aspire for More,

Dr. Tammy, The Catalyst

Global Strategist, Educator, Author, and Speaker

Reading as a Social Action

Reading as a Social and Shared Experience: An Introduction

Tammy C. Francis, Ph.D.

Reading is a process, a complex, interactive, cognitive process that improves with practice (Anderson, Hiebert, Scott, & Wilkinson, 1985; McCormick, 1994; Moore & Hinchman, 2006; NCTE, 2008; Rosenblatt, 1996; Rystrom, 1974; Schoenbach & Greenleaf, 2009; Schoenbach, Greenleaf, Cziko, & Hurwitz, 2000; Weiner, 2009). While there is some uncertainty about how the communicative processes relate to each other, there is a concern that people benefit from opportunities to experience how reading, writing, speaking, and listening support each other (IRA, 2012; NCTE, 2012). The sharing of the reading experience in everyday life does just that; it creates an opportunity to learn. Reading is as much a social act as an academic action.

As a social act, reading can be shared and enjoyed with others. Reading, either reading something oneself or being read to, can convey feelings which potentially evoke both positive and negative emotions. This sharing can have a significant impact on how individuals engage in reading. If reading is seen as being important to significant others in a person's life, that person is more likely to read (Henderson & Berla, 1994; IRA, 2012). At the same time, what an individual chooses to read can also be influenced by other people. This appears to be significant in the case of developing readers. Several researchers have documented the role of a literate environment in fostering literacy development. This aspect, including the modeling and recommendations of significant others, appears to impact the reading of people of all ages.

A series of studies have found that social situations impact a person's reading habits. Pozzer-Ardenghi and Roth (2010) agreed "[r]eading is social practice. We learn it in social situations" (p. 239). Pozzer-Ardenghi and Roth's (2010) review of the literature suggested that students learn and understand more of the concepts "in social situations" involving teachers and peers if students have the opportunity to observe different ways of reading. These can be academic and/or out-of-school reading. Students learn reading habits and practices from their community. As a literacy educator and researcher for more than 24 years, I know this is true for adults as well.

Women Aspiring for More Global Online Reading Community provided an opportunity to inspire and uplift women through reading nonfiction and expository text—creating social interactions and a shared experience around reading and literacy--for women all around the world. My desire for MORE was greater than my reach, larger than Texas, and bolder than the flavor of the best barbeque sauce. Therefore, five years later, we are still thriving on the tenet that reading is a social and shared experience.

References

Anderson, R. C., Hiebert, E. H., Scott, J. A., & Wilkinson, I. A. (1985). *Becoming a nation of readers: The report of the Commission of Reading.* Washington, DC: The National Institute of Education.

Henderson, A. T., & Berla, N. (1994). *A new generation of evidence: The family is critical to student achievement.*

Columbia, MD: National Committee for Citizens in Education.

International Reading Association. (2012). *Adolescent literacy* (Position statement, rev. 2012 ed.). Newark, DE: Author.

McCormick, K. (1994). *The culture of reading and the teaching of English.* New York, NY: Manchester University Press.

Moore, D. W., & Hinchman, K. A. (2006). *Teaching adolescents who struggle with reading.* Boston, MA: Pearson Education, Inc.

National Council of Teachers of English. (2008). Adolescent literacy policy update. Retrieved from http://www.ncte.org/about/issues/national/views/116277.htm.

National Council of Teachers of English. (2012b). Position statement on reading. Retrieved from http://www.ncte.org/positions/statements/positiononreading

Pozzer-Argendhi, L., & Roth, W. (2010). Toward a social practice perspective on the work of reading inscriptions in science texts. Reading Psychology, 31, 228-253. Doi:10.1080/02702710903256361

Rosenblatt, L. M. (1996). *Literature as exploration.* (5th ed.). New York, NY: The Modern Language Association of America.

Schoenbach, R., & Greenleaf, C. L. (2009). Fostering adolescents engaged in academic literacy. In L. Christenbury, R.

Bomer, & P. Smagorinsky (Eds.)., *Handbook of adolescent literacy research* (pp. 98-112). New York, NY: The Guilford Press.

Schoenback, R., Greenleaf, C. L., Cziko, C., & Hurwitz, L. (2000). *Reading for understanding*. San Francisco, CA: Josey-Bass Publishers.

My Journey to Reading

Jeanine Bunzigiye

Since I was five years old, I always read just like my grandpa. I grew up among the old, and there weren't any kids around us expect my twin sister and me. I started developing the love for reading right after my 6th birthday because I was so close to my grandpa. I remembered going to my grandparents' house every day in the afternoon after school and my grandpa used to sit in his balcony and was waiting for my twin sister and I to come. I always ask what book he was reading and what was it all about it. He used to read the newspaper every day. I started asking him to borrow his newspaper to read it for myself.

My grandpa did start challenging me by asking me to read the daily newspaper and to give him a summary. That is how I developed my love for reading. I remembered growing up in a big family and each month it was someone's birth in my family. I came from a family of 14 people and my twin sister and I are the youngest. I started being creative as far as gifts. I started writing poems and wishes cards for every loved one. I didn't have a job, and plus I really believed in being creative and offering what is important which to me it simply showing and expressing the love for my family and friends. It was my mom's birthday one year; I wrote her a poem, and I went and took some flowers in the backyard. She really loved it. Reading has been always the center of my wellbeing. I believe reading and writing goes along especially having a grandpa like mine. My grandpa was always telling me who I am and where I come from. I always had questions for him especially when I saw big words. I didn't hesitate a minute to ask the meaning of it, and I was ready for the next book in his library.

I always find reading and writing fascinating and liberating. Some people have a lot of friends and enjoying people's company all the time. I enjoy reading and writing. If I can start another career now, it would be a writer and teaching people to develop a love for reading--what I enjoy most is the satisfaction it gives me and what it does for my wellbeing. Sometimes when I do get sad, worried, and don't know what to do, reading brings joy, peace, and the knowledge that I need and am looking for. If I can choose an imaginary friend, I will call reading it. In my life, I have been through hardship after hardship and reading has served me well. Reading has been my therapy, my answer to many situations. Reading has been what I really needed to develop my thinking process, learn how to use my voice, and advocate for myself when I had to. Reading has helped shape the person that I am today.

Reading has helped me get empowered by the most powerful leaders in history. I remember growing up in Congo; I heard about Lumumba who was the Prime Minister of the Congo and how he fought of justice in my country. But when I started reading about him in high school and other great leaders, I read to honor my grandpa legacy and to continue the legacy of those men and women that I read in those history book and biographies book. When I couldn't really express myself or wasn't confident about an issue how to go by it. I will just pick a book and start reading.

I always find solutions and empowerment. I will strongly say that reading has been my mentor and my advisor on many levels in my life. And even friends and family members know that Jeanine loves books. Each year, some friends and family members ask me what I want for my birthday; I usually say the same thing, "a gift card to Barnes Noble" because I always have a book that I need to buy since I never get tired of reading. Now, it became a habit of mine every night. I can't go to bed without reading. Or if I am traveling, I can't travel without bringing 2 or 3 books along with me. Books are very important to me, and there was a joke that my family started saying to me. "Jeanine can give you many things but not her books." I came to realize that it was very true, and I always hold on to it for many years since I was in high school until these days.

It was almost impossible for me to bring with me all my books when I was moving from Vermont to North Dakota. In total, I had 10 Boxes full of books, and my mother said, "Jeanine, do you realize that you have more books than clothes?" which in my family or in my culture women tend to have more clothes than books. Everyone was so shocked to see me insisting on not leaving not even one book of mine behind. I did put all those 10 boxes in my car and shipped them. It just goes to show you much I do enjoy reading, and that is my life. I did learn a lot through reading, and I could write books about the impact of reading and how it did and still contributes until these days to my growth as a person, a woman, an educator, an activist, and an entrepreneur.

I start noticing how my nieces, nephew, and friends start always reading just because they noticed how powerful you can be when you do read. It does empower you on another level and expand your mind as well when you do read a lot. To me, it is a very important topic that I can really teach and write for many years to come because reading has tremendously changed my life from when I was 5 years old until these days. And my love for reading grows daily, and I realize it is contagious. I am glad it is because reading is a great tool if you have a message that you want to pass along. I started using my voice just after reading books of great men and women who changed the world and that really transformed my spirit. Since then, I never let a day go by without reading something.

About the Author

Jeanine Bunzigiye is a Global Business strategist, leadership Coach, career coach and Corporate Trainer Consultant and helps people achieve their global goals of growth, global leadership, and implementation as they start their global journey through a purposefully designed program that aids in Global and Leadership development. Jeanine started coaching in 2015 after many years of consulting with different companies and helping them through cultural competency and leadership development through her rich experience as a Global Expert Consultant to inspire others on her journey, Within Her Words. Realizing God was calling her to serve on a higher level, she accepted the call to coach and made a transition into providing powerful, motivational, and transformational programs, products, and services to her target market. Jeanine started serving as Founder and CEO of *With You Solutions* in 2019 to transition her mission and brand to a new level that expanded to reach broader audiences.

Reading Enriches the Mind

Chipo Chitewe

Once upon a time….
There was once….
In the beginning….
Maybe now or never…

However the book starts, it's usually that first page or chapter that determines how long you stick with the story. When you read, you get taken on a journey by the storyteller. Ideally, the writer wants to bring out a certain emotion from the reader through the text. Many a time I have laughed, cried, or been infuriated by the characters in a book. Perhaps these being the emotions the writer was trying to bring out through the characters. I find reading therapeutic. I've always found that when I read, I discover a new world be it fact or fiction I start to see a different view to one picture.

As a lover of books, I've always savoured how the characters create an image in my mind of how they look or how they feel throughout the text. I sort of develop a connection with some and dislike for others often to be met with the biggest twists and turns that leave you so confused and sort of hurt that the character has betrayed you.

This was all from getting engrossed in a good plot. A scene played out so perfectly you get to the end of the book and feel a slight disappointment that the journey with the characters has come to an end.

Think of it as a similar situation to making new friends and having them share their deepest darkest secrets then having to say goodbye before you're ready to move on. This is how reading can make you feel. You then need to pause for a short whilst you reminisce on the journey you've been on with the text before you open up a new world of text.

I recently read a book that took me through a journey that I had to applaud at the end. The moment I had formed a dislike for one character and completely written them off as not being worthy of the pages their story had been written on it turned out that they were the good 'guy' all along.

Wouldn't you love to read a book like that and have someone to bounce the story off? The same way we do with soap operas and movies?

Well, I recently found a love for sharing books. Initially just by book exchange and recommendation but never really getting to discuss the book with anyone.

Then I took up the art of reading as a group, the virtual book club where women were aspiring for more through reading and sharing the adventure of text using our own individual emotions, views, and opinions. Now here is where reading takes a different turn. Suddenly, I had opened up to an art that I would have never otherwise explored. I'd only ever seen book clubs on TV or heard of people who were part of them and met around a room every so often to discuss the books.

Suddenly, I was in one. A book club.

When you read the same text and explore it from different perspectives and different views you begin to open up your thinking to a whole new dimension. Each chapter dissected, analysed and annotated by a different mind. Yet all in all making some sort of sense.

At this point, you begin to realise not only the benefits but the power of coming together. I can only imagine this must be how it was for the world's best architects or designers. Where a bridge is not just a bridge, or a garment is not just a garment. It is a combination of the information taken from several different minds coming together for one purpose.

Well in this same respect, a book is not just a book when you read it together. It is a work of art that brings minds together and develops our thinking collectively to see all the colours of the rainbow. By all the colours of the rainbow I mean, the beauty in our differences.

Reading as a social exercise has not only encouraged me to read more but also set the tone for new friendships and new education. Exploring the text collectively opens up discussions that may otherwise never happen on issues raised within the text. Social reading has made reading a lot more enjoyable for me, and I find that I delight in the opportunity to share my voice in relation to my take aways from the text.

In addition to my love for reading, I now find that I am exploring texts that I would not usually choose in the store and finding that I enjoy them. Widening the genres that I read. There is an openness created when you read as a social exercise because when readers share their take on a text a lot of the time, they share based on a personal experience that they have encountered and show how it relates to the text to create a more relatable view where other readers can immediately understand the angle that the contributor is taking.

Reading as a social exercise enriches the mind, and where you are led by a leader who not only loves reading but teaches reading to adults you find that no matter what level of reading you are. There is so much you can learn not just by reading but by listening to other readers. Feed your imagination by reading more, in the words of Albert Einstein, "Imagination is more important than knowledge. For Knowledge is limited, whereas imagination embraces the entire world, stimulating progress, giving birth to evolution."

I have developed myself more by reading. I have improved my learning by reading. I have become a leader because I read up on what I wanted to teach. More importantly, I have learnt to accept differences through acknowledging a variety of views, methods and thought systems. I encourage you to join *Women Aspiring for More* or find a book club where you can grow.

About the Author

Chipo Chitewe, Mindset Change Motivator, is a Zimbabwean born Accountant based in London holding a Bachelor of Arts Honours Degree in Accounting and Business Information Systems as well as a Professional Qualification with the Chartered Institute of Management Accountants. Chipo is a Published Author and award-winning Speaker.

Founder and CEO of Chipo Chitewe Worldwide Ltd, away from her day job, she is also a Mindset Change Motivation Coach and Speaker serving women through workshops and one to one coaching.

Chipo's passion is teaching women to work in a way that empowers not only them but their child into forward thinking entrepreneurship from a young age, whilst actively achieving their goals. Chipo is a full time working single mother who values communication and connections through speech and leads by her hashtag #Childrenlearnwhattheylive! A firm believer in God Chipo is devoted to being a positive influencer in the world.

Reading Aloud When You're Neurodivergent

Ruth-Ellen Danquah

My earliest conscious memory associated with reading in front of others was covered and drenched in a story fueled with shame. Feeling ashamed that my nostrils would flair whenever I spoke. Feeling ashamed of not being able to articulate my words perfectly. Feeling ashamed that I spoke too fast. This sense of shame didn't derive from nowhere. The shame stemmed from my experiences, like all shame. The shame stemmed from emotions rooted in my subconscious and conscious. Shame much like mold grows in the dark.

I never spoke to anyone about that feeling of shame aloud before and that's how shame starts to dim our light. On the surface I knew I had an issue with reading and believed it was just that incident. But it was a series of incidents that led me to the symptom of not reading in front of others. It's the off the cuff remark like 'I don't understand you', that someone says to you when you read. That off the cuff remark that was said by a stranger who themselves felt something was lacking something in their spirit, so articulated their thoughtless words in order to feel good about themselves. It's a habit that others around us use time and time again in order to reprogram our minds.

Shame can give our lives a shape that is nothing like the shape of the life God desires of for" - Christine Caine (Unashamed)[1]

---

[1] Christine Caine - Unashamed (2016) page 41

Unconsciously reading out loud was anchored with me feeling judged.

I recall a period in college that my college teacher was impressed with and so subsequently asked to read my work in front of others so they could hear why my work got an A. I always had challenges connecting with people and didn't have friends in class, they were more acquaintances. And when I stepped in front of the class, I remember why they were not friends and acquaintances. I could hear one "acquaintance" talk about my how my nose flares when I talked...Then I heard laughter.

I just wanted to get away from the spotlight. I carried this energy of wanting to get away from any attention into my adulthood. I would talk fast in adulthood to get all my words out just in case someone realised I wasn't supposed to be there speaking in the first place. I would decline speaking just in case they noticed that my noise would flair. I would feel unworthy and feel like my words didn't have any value.

It dawned on me one day, that I wasn't reading with the right intentions. It took me years to stop the inner chatter and identify the lies that I had been fed as my truth. The lie that said that I was tolerated. The lie that said I wasn't worthy. And I learnt the truth about strength. That strong people don't put others down, they lift them up.

That is the power of being in a community. A community of women who reinforced that reading with an intention was so empowering. An intention to discuss not judge. An intention to share, not just sit and stare. An intention to move women forward, through the art of connection.

To lead, to participate and knowing when I step into that space, it is sacred and allows for me to connect with people that have similar experiences as me. Knowing that I no longer had to dim my light.

The act of reading in a community became a way for me to empower others to do the same, so that everyone could level up! Reading with intention was a way to anchor my light within. It felt so satisfying to lean into the revelation that dimming my greatness to make others feel comfortable was actually making the world a darker place. It felt so satisfying to bask in the truth that there is nothing wrong with loving your life, even though other people may not love theirs. And even more satisfying to know that loving your life any less will not make others love theirs more, it would just mean that you've joined them in their darkness.

Finding a sisterhood of women for that truth to make common sense a common practice was divine timing. What follows are are some of the light bulbs I experienced when I was leading a reading discussion:

- Reading collectively, reminds each and every single one is great, that your greatness is not a drop in the ocean. You are the entire ocean, in a drop.

- Reading helped me to break free from the shackles of shame.

- All those subconscious and unconscious thoughts that was bubbling beneath the iceberg of my complex mind can got triggered and revealed themselves. I made a conscious decision to bring these thoughts to the surface and no longer, drown part of me.

- Reading collectively was one of the most powerful practices that helped me to honour my thoughts and feelings through connection, instead of dismissing or abandoning myself.

When I read with a group, I always feel that it is something you connect with is a vulnerable act. It's an act that gives you more insight into a piece of you that may be hiding, insight into your true Goddess power. Now the previous statement may sound like a stretch but think about it.

When you take the time to read a book, you commit to at least 4 hours of your time to not only reading words of a book, but to open yourself up to a new way of thinking about life. Gaining a wider perspective and possibly letting go of old ways of thinking. Reading is a just one of the ways to encounter a paradigm shift and step into your power and truth.

I remember cross referencing at least 6 books when I was completing assignments at university, it brought me so much joy to be able to grasp so many different perspectives. And the fact that I could hear all those conversations to bring a richer conversation to the table was amazing.

When you can gain so many different perspectives you are able to improve reading comprehension because you have light bulb moments. 2012 Research by Fibrina Hanung Siswanti[2] showed

[2] https://media.neliti.com/media/publications/61153-EN-the-use-of-small-group-discussion-to-imp.pdf

evidence that small group reading that it improves the readers ability to find finer details and understand main ideas.
That's the great thing about reading, it's like in one book there are thousands of interpretations. I guess that's why bible study is imperative for some groups because you can sometimes miss the message that was meant for you.

With reading in a social setting that happens, your unique voice and perspective picks up something that other people don't. The perspective you have adds value and richness of diversity to a conversation that without your unique voice, would have been missing. But before that can happen you have to be in a place where you are comfortable to share your truth. Your truth sometimes derives from wounds, wounds that need healing. I have learnt that you can't heal your wounds by ignoring them, pushing them down or screaming at them. And when you have healed them and they have turned to scars that you can share, it's doing a disservice to not share your experience, as this helps others to heal their wounds.

You can't play a good hand in life if you're not playing a full deck. You only end up cheating yourself and others of your sheer brilliance. So I learnt that I needed to learn hypnotherapy, NLP. I was dealing with years of shit trauma that was slowly floating the top of the water because I needed to let it stop weighing me down. The lies of not being able to connect with others was a lie. The lies that my voice wasn't important enough to command attention. The lies that dimming my light would help others shine brighter.

An iceberg can serve as a useful (albeit overused) metaphor to understand how much of ourselves we choose to reveal to other people. As an iceberg floats in the water, the huge mass of it remains below the surface. Only a small percentage of the whole iceberg is visible above the surface, and the largest and most influential part remains unseen below the surface.

What follows are two specific books I have read with great intention to help me level up my consciousness and connect with my truth. This levelling up has helped me to step into my power by reinforcing what I needed to hear! Each book has also helped me to be creative and make games out of the learnings, which is a really powerful way to reinforce the message.

How the Motivation Manifesto reminded me that disappointment does not hold power in my story

Disappointment is necessary and holds no real power over us - Brendon Burchard, *The Motivation Manifesto* (2014):

- I used to get so frustrated on a daily basis because I would get up and do what I had to do, but often feel disappointed when I saw little to no progress?
- I have often felt disappointed when I have got up at 6am to go to the gym for 6 months and see no progress in my weight loss.
- I have often felt disappointed when I have been working on making a transformational business and see no progress in my financial situation (despite adding value to people's lives
- I have often felt disappointed when I have put hours into changing my mindset, reconditioning my mind, changing my energy for someone with low energy to undo the work in minutes.

This disappointment has led to my depression, a battle I constantly fight! This disappointment story was not my story! Reading the motivation manifesto helped me to remember that I was paying my dues and the work I are doing NOW would be paid back in full. Disappointment is the gap between reality and expectation. So, you never have to feel disappointed, I want you to do something, give a gift to yourself. I want you to reach out and to ask a friend to help to fortify you so you can feel more encouraged.

I believe no one can give you motivation, it something you generate intrinsically. People can inspire you through their words and actions. But it's knowing your values. Living your values and unapologetically living a value based intentional gangsta life no matter what. Brendon Burchard's *Motivation Manifesto* reminded me of that fact, whenever I am feeling discouraged that I should be a master reframer and come from an empowered place rather than a place of lack. A place of being a contributor not just a consumer. A true place of service. "Let us demand service...Those without this virtue in their hearts must not be within our circle. Remove them at once, as the selfish and the unconcerned will rip us from glory" - *The Motivation Manifesto* - Brendon Burchard (2014).

In the women's book group, we read the *Motivation Manifesto* years after I purchased it and it reinforced the message that I believe God reminds me of daily to direct my energy to make a difference. "The work is great and extensive, and we are separated on the wall far from one another." Nehemiah 4:19

It wasn't just Burchard who reminded me to be a master reframer. Shonda Rhimes's *Year of Yes: How to Dance It Out, Stand In the Sun and Be Your Own Person* was edifying literature.

How Shonda Yes, taught me to Say the word no more
When we read Shonda's book YES! as a group I was determined not only who to say yes to, but also to who and what I say no to. My no list is often much longer than my yes list now days.

An effective way for me to do this is to have a personal manifesto (reinspired by Brendon). This manifesto would help to support me stay focused, so if anything comes into my realm that isn't in alignment to that manifesto, I can say no. Then like a conveyor belt process I decide where it goes on my list:

Do it now
Defer
Delegate
Delete

How I learnt this lesson
I used to run monthly workshops for people with dyslexia every month for 7+ years. Some of the people I encountered were not ready to take responsibility for the part they played in their life choices. One guy who thought it was my duty to help "fix him". As you know, we can't fix anyone, because no one is broken.

I learnt that without boundaries people will have misguided expectations, which you can't blame them for because it's up to us to create our boundaries and make it clear. It's up to us to manage their expectations. I make it clear what I tolerate, make it plain, remind them and have consequences that you actually follow through if they don't stick to it.

Recently, a guy I was dating, fat shamed me. I decided to not put up with it and made it clear we would not be moving forward in communication. To some, it may sound rigid, but we must remember our worth. We are not here to be used and abused by people, if we believe that we are, we will start disconnecting from the world.

Managing expectations on both sides by setting clear boundaries (and optimising them as you go) will do wonders for your overall peace of mind and stop those frustrating awkward moments. When people show you (not tell you) who they are believe them, they are honest in their actions. It's up to us to then make a decision as to whether we want that type of energy in our life.

Years later after starting my company, *Celebrated Not Tolerated,* I can connect the dots and see that I have always had compassion for people that was excluded from the popular table. When I worked in corporate, I found myself being the one of two black people in the whole company. I knew about social cues before it became a thing and connected with me soon to be boss by talking about things you weren't supposed to.

It's not just about reading because if the forgetful curve can teach us anything, it's that we must intentionally use the information in order for it to be useful. Reading with an intention helps you to get present so you can hear the message that is being revealed by your subconscious. By revealing those subconscious thoughts that are sabotaging you, you are able to denounce those limiting beliefs, clear your abundance blocks, so you can accept yourself instead of rejecting yourself.

About the Author

Ruth-Ellen Danquah is a mother of two, who was identified with dyslexia, dyspraxia, autism and ADHD in her later 30's and has been working in the neurodiversity space for over 9 years.
She is an author and professional speaker on neurodiversity at work, as well as the Chief Innovation Officer for a leading neurodiversity social enterprise based in the UK. She is an accredited consultant, trainer & certified life coach, business coach, NLP Master Practitioner & holds a diploma in DBT.

She believes we all should be celebrated not just tolerated. In her own company, *Celebrated Not Tolerated,* she works as a trainer & consultant helping HR professionals & EDI teams to build neuro-inclusive workplaces so everyone can belong and feel celebrated not just tolerated.

Renewing the Spark for Reading

LaShun Gaines

My passion to read was sparked,
By reading a great work of art.
Engaged in what the author penned,
Captured my attention from start to end.
The passion burned in me to talk,
With like-minded souls about my thoughts.
Community, creativity, and connection ignited,
New perspectives and views, my mind was enlightened.
I have never saw it from that angle before,
Jotting down insights and returning to read more.
Empowered to READ ON, I'll continue to dream,
Reading, writing, and sharing new things!

I love to read! Learning to read continues to be an empowering experience. A good book can get you talking! Reading a good book provokes you to want to share your experiences with some else. An interesting read captures the mind and draws you into the action. Relaxing and curling into a good book can ease the mind and heart. It sparks passion, engaging all five senses, and expands your world! Just like a cutting-edge TV series, reading will keep you coming back for more and more! Although reading is a fairly isolated and independent action, it can be enhanced by connections, community, perspective, brain power, passion and creativity through human conversations.

Connections

From personal experiences to the world we live in, connections make reading a more engaging experience. Readers make connections with the text and world during isolated independent times. Reading becomes a more enjoyable experience and is enhanced when shared in collaboration with others. Making connections socially and with various aspects of the text heightens the literary experience. Sharing a story about a past experience leads to another person connecting and sharing something that happened to them. Adult learners are more self-directed and bring a vast amount of prior knowledge when making connections to literacy text (Knowles, 1975). In the act of sharing these connections, social bonds begin to form as you learn more about yourself and others. Sometimes connections made with the text may be positive or a pivotal moment. Pivotal moments provoke thought and reflection, prompting you to journal or as Dr. Tammy would say, "do the work", to explore more about yourself. New insights may develop causing a release of an old way of thinking to a new way of thinking.

Community

Reading and engaging with other readers provide a network within a community. Within the community, trust is being built to allow all members to feel safe sharing rich personal and professional experiences. You are more apt to engage with other readers, even if it is your first time to meet them. Everyone has a sense of belonging to the group and knows their contribution is heard, felt and valued. At some point, readers affirm one another increasing support for one another. I am able to hear other women's experiences and their perspectives on handling them. In the safe space, the discussion may lead to deeper layers of the same topic as more readers chime in and share.

Building community and engaging other readers enable all women to socially engage and grow personally and professionally. Staying abreast of your profession is by far one of the leading and essential tasks of leaders in their profession. Engaging in the latest and greatest practices keeps one up to date with cutting edge practices in their profession. Engaging in collegial dialogue allows women to become informed practitioners to empower others with the leading practices in their profession. Listening, turning to one another causes comprehension of text to increase in the minds of readers.

Perspective

Perspective is the way in which you look at something. Further, perspective is an attitude or feeling about the way we view something. Reading broadens perspective and expands understanding of the themes, characters, and events of the text. It is extremely amazing how two different people who may see the same thing can have different ways of viewing it! The opportunity to share connections made with the text, enlighten individuals to another's perspective. Not only can you share a text-to-text connection, but a spiritual or emotional connection with other souls who share the same passion for reading. Some notions read in various texts challenge you to think differently and change a fixed mindset to a growth mindset. I am enlightened to ways I can hone my craft and expand my dreams. Engaging other readers' perspectives of the same stories and ideas you independently responded to prior to the discussion.

Brain power and reduced stress

Did you know that reading sharpens the brain? According to brain research, reading stimulates connectivity in the brain. Engaging in reading encourages mental enrichment and exercise. New research suggests that learning to read does more than make life easier: it literally changes how the brain works by increasing connectivity between its regions (Pierre-Louis, 2017). No matter what type of book you read, you are giving your brain a workout every time you turn each page. Stress disappears when you grab a book and read, forgetting about anything that may be bothering you. Researchers note that engaging in reading six minutes during the day slows heart rates and reduces tension (Hampton, 2018). Reading helps me to unwind, recharge and destress, which is a blessing to our greatest wealth, our health!

Passion and Creativity

Reading sparks passion and creativity! As you engage and listen to others during book talk, you begin to think about what others are sharing. Listening to their perspective causes you to think about things that you have not thought about before. You may jot down a thought in your journal to explore after book talk or something new you want to incorporate into your daily routine. Engaging in book talk stretches my thinking beyond ideas I initially set out to discuss. Margaret Wheatley states, if we sit together and talk about what is important to us, we begin to come alive (Wheatley, 2002). Whether you are penning ideas for writing your own books, poems or new intriguing ideas for your business, creativity soars when sharing with others.

Reading with others has changed my reading habits, reading experiences, reading enjoyment, and/or attitude toward reading for publication. Limited time often leads to a neglect for the things you love. During the coronavirus pandemic, I have more time to devote to reading and join in book discussions. I also read professionally with my team at work. Reading empowers my ability as a Bible teacher to weave connections and spark discussions with adult learners. My habit of picking up a book has increased, and I look forward to sharing ideas with others. I have read books that I would not choose myself. I enjoy listening to other women's perspectives and have found areas of agreement, as well as new ideas to explore. Reading a book can lead to life-changing experiences, not just a simple pleasure of a one-time read!

References

Knowles, M. (1975). *Self-Directed Learning*. Chicago: Follet.

Berns Gregory S., et al., "Short- and Long-Term Effects of a Novel on Connectivity in the Brain," Brain Connectivity, December 2013; 3(6):590-600. Retrieved from: http://online.liebertpub.com/doi/abs/10.1089/brain.2013.0166.

Pierre-Louis, Kendra. (2017) *Learning to read as an adult might change the way your brain works*. Retrieved from: https://www.popsci.com/adult-reading-brain/

Heavenridge, Paul. (2015). *Literacy works: Why Read? Reason #6: Knowledge is power, but imagination is more valuable*. Retrieved from: www.literacyworks.org

Hampton, Debbie. (2018). *Seven Ways Reading Benefits your Brain*. Retrieved from: https://thebestbrainpossible.com/reading-improves-brain-memory-stress/

Wheatley, Margaret. (2002). *Turning to One Another: Simple Conversations to Restore Hope to the Future*. San Francisco, CA: Berrett-Koehler Publishers, Inc.

About the Author

Mrs. LaShun Gaines is a wife, mother, minister, Bible teacher, and educator. Mrs. Gaines earned a Bachelor of Arts degree from Texas Southern University in Houston, Texas with a major in Sociology and a minor in English. LaShun earned a Master of Arts degree from Southwest Texas State University in San Marcos, Texas with a major in Elementary Education and a cognate in Reading. She served as a District 504/Dyslexia/RTI Coordinator in Elgin ISD for more than 5 years. She currently serves as Early Intervention Coordinator in the Hays CISD Curriculum and Instruction Academic Support Department. LaShun has a total of 23 years of service as an educator and administrator. LaShun lives in Buda, Texas and is married to Jason Gaines, Sr. LaShun and Jason have three children, DeAndre, Jayla, and Jason Jr.

My Journey to Self-love through Reading

Lynn Kanyowa-Ndhlovu

Reading has always been something I started from a very young age. I used to pick up a novel and bury myself in the story, live it, feel the emotions being conveyed by the author and I enjoyed every minute of it. To me reading is a solitary pleasure something to savour curled up on the sofa, big cup of tea and rich tea biscuits. My obsession of reading was fueled one day when I picked up a book by Susan Lewis called Dance whilst you can. I became obsessed with reading fictional novels, I was reading a book all the time, even at work on my break I was buried in a book.

Over eight years ago, I joined network marketing. I was introduced to personal development or self-help books. It took a while for me to really get into them because I was used to reading fictional books. The emotions I was getting were different I was starting to get positive, the way I was viewing the world started to change and I started to believe more in myself and the goals I wanted to achieve. Things changed when I joined Women Aspiring for More book club. This is where we pick a book every month and members review the book chapter by chapter and we share our takeaways.

Before I joined WAM, I never thought of group reading before. If a book was difficult for me to understand or read (there are some books that are complex), I would just drop it maybe never to read it again. This is exactly what happened when we were reading "Ask and it is given" by Esther and Jerry Hicks. It's one of those books I neither could understand nor absorb, but some women had read the book, and some were reading it for the first time and were enjoying it. The reviews, feedbacks, and takeaways from the book helped me to really understand the book, I started to see it from a different perspective and has become one of my favourite books. I love it when they say your greatest gift is your happiness. "The greatest gift that you could ever give to another is your own happiness, for when you are in a state of joy, happiness or appreciation you are fully connected to the stream of pure positive Source Energy that is truly who you are." I love this because I might have all that I desire, I might travel, have a big house and the best lifestyle but without happiness it all means nothing. Being happy and grateful with what you have is what makes life rich. Happiness is everything in life fulfilment and when you share that happiness with others they benefit too. I can confidently share ideas and reviewing books together does help and make the book easier to understand.

I can confidently say being part of WAM has played a part in my growth in personal development. This growth has helped me to handle the pressures that come with continuous changes, challenges, tasks and setting goals. It's not about certain areas of my life but all of them. My desire was to excel, in all areas of my life but that doesn't happen overnight and certainly with a negative mindset. I was so negative. I blamed everyone else but me for not excelling in my network marketing business. For instance, I would think family and friends don't support me, nobody likes to buy from me, it's the products, it's my team, it's everybody else but me. Once I started to invest in personal development, most of which happened through WAM, I realised I was the main problem. Self-doubt does kill dreams and it kills your vibe and blinds you from seeing your true potential. One thing for sure, I was the problem and that needed to be fixed before I totally self-destruct.

Being part of this group and reading with others helped me from being negative Nancy to positive Patty. I have shifted my thinking; my priorities and I have shifted my focus from all the things going wrong to how can I improve and be better than what I was yesterday. I definitely attribute my personal development to WAM community.

Reading with others in WAM has become a huge part of my life, as we are always reading personal development books. This has created a strong community that supports, encourages, and uplifts one another. I noticed that whatever book we read, it always triggered past experiences and challenges. What best way to learn than the power of a life experience story, it's more relatable and people are prone to listen and learn from it. Hearing other women's stories made me realise that I can be anything I want to be in life. I have power and control of my life and I hold the key to all the events that happens in it. The power of a community is you learn from each other's mistake, you pass on knowledge and exchange tips and ideas. This was very instrumental in believing in myself, the thought that other women valued my opinion and my take onboard my contributions. Who wouldn't want to be part of that community?

I truly enjoy reading with others in WAM because this has allows us to learn from each other and help us to being more interactive with each other enabling us to open up and be more self-confident. I have made connections with some amazing women in the group. We might not be able to meet physical needs, but we support the emotional needs we carry through life. As the Bible say in Galatians 6 verse 2, carry each other's burdens and in this way, you will fulfil the law of Christ. We are supporting one another in hard times and carry one another's burdens. It makes it easy for me and others to have the courage to ask when we are the ones in need of support, prayer or need a shoulder to cry on. I have had the privilege to meet Dr. Tammy, who is the founder of WAM. She has also become my mentor, a friend and supports me emotionally too. This is more than a community; it's a sisterhood that allows you to let your light shine. In a world where women are constantly putting each other down it's so refreshing to be part of something that encourages you to sparkle.

Social reading especially being part of WAM has had an impact in my life. I now challenge myself to always perform my best and never doubt my abilities. I have constantly stepped outside my comfort zone as a business owner and life in general. I am a better person than what I was before I joined in the group, and I'm more positive about life.

Reading with others allows you to share experiences, learn from each other's challenges and wins too. Personal development and personal growth are an ongoing process, one that is lifelong. We are constantly learning new things every day and having that knowledge gives you the power to be in control of all aspect of your life. Sharing this learning and growth with other women makes it worthwhile and exciting too. I have found my tribe, and we love each other very hard.

About the Author

Lynn Kanyowa-Ndhlovu is an Instagram Marketing Strategist, and she help startup entrepreneurs to market and scale their brands on IG using simple strategies. She was born in Zimbabwe but currently lives in London with her husband and son. When she finished High School in the UK, she pursued a nursing career which has helped shape the person she is today.

She also does charity work with different organisations, such as the one million pad campaign that raised sanitary pads for women in Africa. She is a board member of The TeamCaro Foundation which provides support to those diagnosed or living with cancer. She has been recognised and received three awards for her efforts to create a positive culture and supporting other women in their endeavours.

Follow her on Instagram @lynnkofficial and
Facebook: Lynn Kanyowa-Ndhlovu

Birthing Beauty through Reading

Shawntai Lister-Mitchell

At an early age, I've always had an infatuation with perfumes, bubble baths, bath oils, and all things considered "girly, prissy and feminine." I remember going through my mother Juanita, grandmother Henri, Marie, aunt Deborah, and great aunt Mattie's perfumes and AVON products. I loved the various smells of the perfumes, the unique shapes of the bottles and the joy of experiencing the vast aromas, as I sprayed the perfume on my neck and wrist.

The passion from my childhood love grew and could not be contained. From this love, I started a natural beauty brand, Class and Elegance Bath and Body Care, LLC. I've been able to hand-craft an array of products for family, friends and what some may call customers or clients, I call my CEBBC family. Through the gift of reading, I've been able to find nuggets of wisdom to assist me on this great journey of discovery. I've created oatmeal baths to help ease the itching and discomfort of eczema for a family member to a facial/body salve that assisted a child-hood friend, who was in a motorcycle accident. The gift of reading has afforded me the opportunity to network with other business owners, advocates, non-profit organizations, women empowerment groups/communities, and to learn about the benefits of aromatherapy and so much more. Reading has also enriched my life with new friends and helped me to reacquaint myself with old friends in the WAM Reading Community. One of my most memorable experiences, was the opportunity to share what I've learned through reading and research on the Huffington Post UK, with a co-authored collaboration.

Sisterhood - WAM Connections
Once of the books we discussed in WAM closely relates to me following my passion, dreams, and purpose. *Gifts of Imperfection* by Brené Brown was the first book read in the group. I was honored and excited to be the first member to go live in the Facebook community to discuss the book. I was able to discuss the book and encourage the WAM community to let go of what people think. Our first discussion from the book was Guidepost #1: Cultivating Authenticity – Letting Go of What People Think. I was also able to later discuss Guidepost #9: Cultivating Meaningful Work – Letting Go of Self Doubt and Supposed To. Authenticity is defined as quality of being authentic. Some of the synonyms of authenticity or authentic are genuineness, legitimacy, trustworthiness, credibility, accuracy and my all-time favorite synonym, "truth".

It is vital we walk in our truth in this life's journey. Without truth, there is no authenticity in who we are and we not only do ourselves a discredit but it is a disservice to all the people who are in need of our God given gifts and talents. I believe we are created by God and for God for a purpose. Remember our gifts are to share with others to assist them, encourage them, build them up, teach them, guide them, lead them, etc...

During the discussion of Guidepost #9: Cultivating Meaningful Work – Letting God of Self Doubt and Supposed To, we were able to share our personal interpretation of meaningful work. My question to you is, "What is your meaningful work?". Some refer to it as "your calling", "purpose", "making a difference", "leaving the world a better place than you found it" and "existence for living". The beautiful thing about your life story is you can have several expressions of meaningful work at different stages or seasons in your life. Embrace all of you, including your joy, pain, perceived failure, disappointments, teachings, knowledge, wisdom, kindness, distractions, imperfections, inconsistencies, insecurities, love, and all that encompasses you and your journey.

Motivation and Affirmations

One thing that really touches my heart is the way the women in the WAM community and other communities I'm apart of or have been a part of, encourage one another. One of my passions is to encourage women by speaking, teaching, sharing my knowledge and resources and being as transparent as I can be. Give all of you in everything you do. Don't be afraid to share with the world who you truly are. Daily affirmations have been a dear, close friends to me. They've enabled me to lift myself up when I was going through difficult times, when I was uncertain of the value within me. Whether it was an affirming scripture, mantra or saying, I've embraced them and made them apart of my daily living. One way I've incorporated my passion of encouragement is through affirming and motivating labels on my product line. It gives me great joy to collaborate with words that plant seeds of kindness, hope, love, remembrance of self and positive energy.

Affirm Thyself and Others

It's an honor to share with you the affirming messages I've included on several of my products with you in mind.

1. **Forgive, Love and BEE Kind.** If you'll notice, I spelled be as "bee". This concept was created when formulating my Chamomile Orange Lip Balm. I love supporting local producers, crafters and farmers and use local honey and beeswax (when available) in the product. The act of

forgiveness is always an act of kindness to yourself in addition to others. Forgiveness heals the soul and body. It frees the body of heaviness and in some way is a spiritual enema. Yes, I said enema. Forgiveness cleanses the body of toxins and allows us to take in and absorb the beautiful things in life we need to bring healing, such as love and understanding.

2. **Remember, you are beautiful.** So many times in life we are unable to see clearly the beauty we possess. Not only physical beauty but true beauty, radiating from within. We often mistake of failures or perceived failures, insecurities and doubts as a reflection of the beauty we possess. In my opinion, true beauty is embracing all of you, the entire rose. The stem, thorns, leaves and petals of the flower, all serve a purpose. Roses are strong yet soft, beautiful, and radiant and so are you.

3. **Smile, Love and Encourage Others**. A smile is a simple gesture that can bring great joy to someone. Think about all the challenging and difficult moments in life you kept to yourself. Think about the person who smiled at you. It could be a friend, family member, co-worker or stranger. Think about how it made you feel. It's something about a smile that can lift your spirit and the spirits of others. I specifically remember times in my life, when I received words of encouragement from someone, who was unaware of the turmoil happening to me internally. Those words of encouragement reminded me I was not alone in this journey and confirmed I could indeed go on.

4. **Embrace your unique beauty**. I often bask in the wonder and awe of God and his creation. On road trips, my husband knows

I'm going to marvel at the beauty of nature, especially trees, mountains, and rocks. I am also in awe of our own unique beauty. We are unique beings, and although we may possess similar features, there is no one else on this planet like you. Think about it for a minute. There are billions of people in the world, and no one has your exact DNA, eye shape, strands of hair, shape, sound of voice or hue. This should let you know how beautiful you are. When we learn to embrace unique beauty, we allow ourselves to be more open and accepting.

5. **Change the world with love**. This is a simple truth, yet many do not understand. We do not have to agree with everything to be loving. Love is being kind, respectful, accepting, embracing differences, learning, and empathizing with others, sharing your story, listening to the stories and journeys of others and respecting your truth and the truth of others.

6. **You are one of a kind.** There is no one like you in the world. That is what I call a self-esteem booster.

7. **You are a gift to the world.** I've often said the most gifts and talents reside in the cemetery. So many times, we bury our most precious gift and allow the pains and experiences of this world to dictate who we are. You are the best gift you can give someone. You in all your beauty, authenticity and flaws wrapped in an exquisite package. Ask yourself, what gifts to you have to share with the world. Is it the gift of loving, smiling, empathizing, cooking, sewing, baking, teaching, learning, sharing, encouraging, motivating? Whatever your gift or gifts are, do not allow them stay buried within.

This is your call to action. Please share with me on Facebook, Instagram, and Twitter how you daily affirm yourself and use the hashtag #cebbcaffirm and tag and follow us on our social media platforms at @cebathbody.

About the Author

Shawntai Lorraine Lister-Mitchell, the wife of Lloyd Shelton Mitchell, daughter of Lloyd and Juanita Lister, sister of Daniel Lister and proud mother of Unique Lister, is a native of Corpus Christi, Texas and currently resides in Mississippi. She has been a part of the beauty industry for over twenty years. She holds a bachelor's degree in Business Administration and has worked with major cosmetics and skincare companies. Lady Shawntai is the owner and founder of Class and Elegance Bath and Body Care, LLC, an herbal and aromatherapy-based brand that meticulously crafts products to transform your bath, body, and skincare needs. Many of the products are made using herbal infusions and ancient remedies. She also loves to encourage women and partner with mentor academies, non-profits, and other organizations to talk about the importance of using and making natural bath, body, and skin care products.

The WAM Book Review Template

D. Trifanya Osei

THE WAM REVIEW

TITLE OF THE BOOK: ______________________

NAME OF AUTHOR: ______________________

PRINTING DATE ______________________

FICTION OR NON-FICTION ______________________

I. SUMMARY OF THE BOOK

____

____

____

____

____

____

II. STRENGTHS OF THE BOOK

____

____

____

____

____

____

III. WEAKNESSES OF THE BOOK

IV. RECOMMENDATION

About the Author

D. Trifanya Osei, affectionately known as Elegant Granny, is a Restoration Strategist with 35 years of experience in the healthcare industry, 20 years as a private school educator, and 9 years as business owner and operator.

Through her business, Elegant Granny LLC, she helps survivors of abuse heal and restore from traumatic experiences. Osei is also creator and host of the Proactive Eye podcast discussing topics of intimate partner violence (domestic violence), child abuse, sexual violence and sexual assault, and suicide prevention as it relates to abuse.

Osei is currently a doctoral candidate in Business Administration specializing in Social Impact Management. In addition, she is an Author, Poet, Usui Reiki Master Practitioner, and Activist for victims of abuse.

Website: https://linkr.bio/ElegantGranny

Afterword

Legacy. It is my hope that this book will serve as a way to create a lasting legacy for the ladies in my community. My platform is designed to empower others on their journey toward more.

My philosophy and brand are centered on educating, empowering, and equipping others while exploring who we are, where we are going, and other places around the world. Therefore, being intentional and mind set work are tantamount to making our dreams a reality.

Catalyst 4 Change Global is an educational consulting firm that empowers Black and Brown communities with the tools, strategies, and resources necessary to move in the direction of more and be successful in life and business. To make a global impact and serve as a catalyst 4 change in all aspects of our community, education, and business. To effect change globally in education, literacy, college and career readiness, business, entrepreneurship, leadership, and personal sovereignty.

I explain my company and brand because this group, this book, these stories are ways in which we are being catalysts for change in and of our communities.

Did I mention legacy? Children learn reading habits and practices from their community. A major component in language and literacy development is parental involvement and the literacy events that occurs in a child's home environment. Children from a home with a high degree of literacy and parents who engage in intentional oral and literate acts (i.e., speaking to the child, playing word games with the child, reading, writing, and purposefully engaging the child in those acts) develop higher levels of both oral language and literacy. Purcell-Gates (1996) conducted a descriptive study of the literacy practices of 20 lower socio-income families. Within these 20 families, she measured the literacy knowledge of 24 children, ages four to six. The results strongly suggested that a pattern of relationships existed between home literacy practices and a child's emergent literacy knowledge. Those children whose parents engaged in intentional reading had higher measures of literacy both at home and in school.

We are passing this on to our daughters, sons, sisters, brothers, cousins, and friends. We hope you will pick up a book, read it, and share it with other women as well as little girls. Give them what they need to aspire for more, be more, have more, and do more.

Empower. Educate. Equip. Explore.

Share a selfie with your favorite book or a book on your reading or "TBR" list. Be creative. Share a little about who you are and a story or comment about how reading with others has changed your reading habits, reading experience(s), reading enjoyment, and/or attitude toward reading.

On social media post, use the hashtags:
#raasaproject #c4cglobal1 #readingasasocialaction #wamraasa #wam #drtammyfrancis

Reference

Purcell-Gates, V. (1996). Stories, coupons, and *TV Guide*: Relationship between home literacy experiences and emergent literacy knowledge. *Reading Research Quarterly, 31* (4), 406-428.

Artwork: Marcus Humose @humarte

About the Editor and Founder

Tammy Francis, Ph.D., The Catalyst, is a Texas native. Affectionately called Dr. Tammy, she is the CEO and founder of Catalyst 4 Change Global, LLC and the C4C Global Community. Dr. Tammy has a Ph.D. in Curriculum and Instruction. Currently, Dr. Tammy is a tenured Associate Professor at a community college in Texas. She also teaches blockchain courses at Althash University, a global campus that offers online blockchain programs. Additionally, she serves as the Director of Curriculum, Instruction, Certification, and Accreditation with International Council of Registered Blockchain Professionals (ICORBP).

Moreover, Dr. Tammy is a global strategist, consultant, author, and speaker. Dr. Tammy's areas of research and expertise are literacy education, curriculum and instruction, college and career readiness, business, entrepreneurship, blockchain technology, and technology innovation in education. As an edupreneur, she empowers and equips leaders, entrepreneurs, and business startups all over the world with purpose-driven, creative business solutions. Additionally, she provides education on the new literacies, multiliteracies, future of work, and careers in the blockchain, Web 3.0, and digital assets industries. Dr. Tammy also creates blockchain educational programs and certifies blockchain professionals and blockchain programs, institutions, and organizations around the world.

As an entrepreneur and strategist, Dr. Tammy helps purpose driven leaders move in the direction of more and prepare for what's next by providing the tools and strategies needed to plan and live on purpose. She also offers goal setting/vision sessions, purpose planning workshops, and conscious connections retreats. Dr. Tammy inspires others on their journey toward more while sharing hers and facilitating conversations in her *Women Aspiring for More* and *Catalyst 4 Change Global Online Reading Communities*.

As an educator for more than 20 years, Dr. Tammy has taught in the K-12 and higher education classrooms. Dr. Tammy helps adults improve their reading and writing skills as well as their ability to be successful in college and life. She offers her services as a consultant and professional developer to support educators in the secondary and postsecondary classroom to improve reading and writing instruction across the curriculum as well as student success strategies in the school setting. She also shares instructional strategies that create an engaged, equitable, and inclusive environment for students from diverse backgrounds.

She has served and currently serves on several local, national, and international boards. She has also been recognized with many professional awards for her contributions to the field of education, research, and entrepreneurship.

To connect with Dr. Tammy and participate in a transformational experience, you can join one of the many opportunities she has for you to engage in a cocoon experience or follow her across all social media platforms @DrTammyFrancis. You can follow her community @C4CGlobal1 or visit www.catalyst4changeglobal.net.

DrTammyFrancis.com

Email: info@drtammyfrancis.com

APPENDIX

Artwork: Marcus Humose @humarte

Appendix A

About the Artist

Marcus Humose is a creative. He is an artist and actor. He started pursuing an acting career back in 2019. He has done multiple short films with the students at the Florida State University film school. They were able to help him establish his foundation as an actor. Marcus has acquired a bank of knowledge from working with them. His ultimate goal is to be a working full-time actor.

His headshots and resumé are available upon request.

Vimeo link:
https://vimeo.com/humarte

Appendix B

Booklist

Appendix C

The WAM Book Review Templates

THE WAM REVIEW

TITLE OF THE BOOK: ____________________

NAME OF AUTHOR: ____________________

PRINTING DATE ____________________

FICTION OR NON-FICTION ____________________

I. SUMMARY OF THE BOOK

____

____

____

____

____

____

II. STRENGTHS OF THE BOOK

____

____

____

____

____

____

III. WEAKNESSES OF THE BOOK

IV. RECOMMENDATION

THE WAM REVIEW

TITLE OF THE BOOK:

NAME OF AUTHOR:

PRINTING DATE

FICTION OR NON-FICTION

I. SUMMARY OF THE BOOK

II. STRENGTHS OF THE BOOK

III. WEAKNESSES OF THE BOOK

IV. RECOMMENDATION

THE WAM REVIEW

TITLE OF THE BOOK: ____________

NAME OF AUTHOR: ____________

PRINTING DATE ____________

FICTION OR NON-FICTION ____________

I. SUMMARY OF THE BOOK

____

____

____

____

____

____

II. STRENGTHS OF THE BOOK

____

____

____

____

____

____

III. WEAKNESSES OF THE BOOK

IV. RECOMMENDATION

THE WAM REVIEW

TITLE OF THE BOOK: ________________

NAME OF AUTHOR: ________________

PRINTING DATE ________________

FICTION OR NON-FICTION ________________

I. SUMMARY OF THE BOOK

II. STRENGTHS OF THE BOOK

III. WEAKNESSES OF THE BOOK

IV. RECOMMENDATION

THE WAM REVIEW

TITLE OF THE BOOK: ______________________

NAME OF AUTHOR: ______________________

PRINTING DATE ______________________

FICTION OR NON-FICTION ______________________

I. SUMMARY OF THE BOOK

____

____

____

____

____

____

II. STRENGTHS OF THE BOOK

____

____

____

____

____

____

III. WEAKNESSES OF THE BOOK

IV. RECOMMENDATION